YOUR KNOWLEDGE HAS VALUE

Bibliographic information published by the German National Library:

The German National Library lists this publication in the National Bibliography; detailed bibliographic data are available on the Internet at http://dnb.dnb.de .

Imprint:

Copyright © 2014 GRIN Verlag, Open Publishing GmbH
Print and binding: Books on Demand GmbH, Norderstedt Germany
ISBN: 978-3-656-72175-8

This book at GRIN:

http://www.grin.com/en/e-book/278662/problems-of-gender-accord-of-two-gender-noun-determiners

Xhafer Beqiraj

Problems of gender accord of two-gender noun determiners

GRIN Publishing

GRIN - Your knowledge has value

Since its foundation in 1998, GRIN has specialized in publishing academic texts by students, college teachers and other academics as e-book and printed book. The website www.grin.com is an ideal platform for presenting term papers, final papers, scientific essays, dissertations and specialist books.

Visit us on the internet:

http://www.grin.com/

http://www.facebook.com/grincom

http://www.twitter.com/grin_com

Xhafer Beqiraj

Problems of gender accord of two-gender noun determiners

Language phenomenon of two-gender (heterogeneous) nouns, which appears in some Indo-European languages, has for a long time drawn attention of linguists. This phenomenon appeared in languages such as: French, Italian, Romanian, Slovakian, Czech and Albanian, as for example:

> it. *il labbro (sg. m.)* – *le labbra (pl. f.)* "*një buzë – disa buzë*";
>
> fr. *l'amour (sg. m.)* – *les amours (pl. f.)* "*një dashuri – disa dashuri*";
>
> rum. *osul (sg. m)* – *oasele (pl. f.)*[1] "*një kockë – disa kocka*";
>
> al. *një mendim (sg. m.)* – *disa mendime (pl. f.)[a thought); djathë (sg. m)* –
>
> *djathëra (pl. f.) [cheese].*

In each of these languages, nouns of this category in singular are of masculine gender, but in plural they are transformed into feminine gender. This is known as two-gender phenomenon. Nouns which are classified into this category, denominate mainly non animated beings, things or abstract notions, such as: *element-i element-e* (element) *vend-i* – *vend-e* (place), *qytet-i* – *qytet-e* (city) *kryeqytet-i* – *kryeqytet-e* (capital city), *breg-u* – *brigj-e* (hill), *lloj-i* – *lloj-e* (type), *send-i* – *send-e* (thing), *djep-i* – *djepe* (cradle), etc; *vaji* - *vajra* (oil), *fshat-i* –*fshatra* (village), *debat-i* - *debat-e*[2] (debate), *drithë-i* – *drithëra* (corn) *ujë-i* - *ujëra,*

---

[1] http://www.de.wikipedia.org/wiki/Genus#Ambigeneratjen.
[2] Wilfried Fiedler, *Die Pluralbildung im Albanischen*, ASHAK, Prishtinë, 2007, p. 213.

1

(water), *lesh-i – leshra* (wool)), *mall-i - mallra* (goods), *të qeshura* (laughs)[3] etc.

In this category are also some nouns which denominate human beings, such as; *personazh-personazhe* (character), *ekipazh-ekipazhe* (crew), *personalitet-personalitete* (personality), *ekip-ekipe* (team), *insekt-insekte* (insect), *bakter-baktere* (bacteria), *virus-viruse* (virus), *mikrob-mikrobe* (microbe) etc. So in Albanian language two-gender nouns are those of masculine gender (a group of which primarily were of neuter gender) which form the plural by adding suffixes **–e** and **–ra**.

In Albanian grammar, this category of nouns was problematic, as for the gender of adjective determiners which should be taken in plural. In lecturing practice we encounter both: an adjective in feminine gender and in masculine gender as well. This was pointed out for the first time by Sami Frashëri, who in his work "Shkronjëtorja" states that there are few nouns of masculine gender with both masculine and feminine gender in plural, such as: *ky mal – këta male* or *këto male* (this mountain – these mountains); *ky emër–këta emra* or *këto emra*[4] (this noun - these nouns).

We find the treatment of this phenomenon in the grammar book of I. D. Sheper, Father J. Rrota , K. Cipo etc. A special dedication to this study was made by prof. Shaban Demiraj in his work titled: *"Rreth ndërrimit të gjinisë së emrave në shumës në shqipe vështruar edhe në përqasje me rumanishten"* ("About the gender change of nouns in plural in Albanian language, with a view and comparison with Romanian language", Sh. Demiraj) in which he has seen two - gender nouns in Albanian, from the diachronic and synchronic point of view, but also in comparison with some Indo-European languages. According to him, this phenomenon is relatively old (preliteral) and has to do with an inner development of Albanian language, denying the influence of Romanian and

---

[3] W. Fideler: "Ich habe bereits an anderer Stelle ausfrührlich gezeigt, daß die Wörter, die im Singular mask. sind, im modernen Albanischen speziell des Untersuchungszeitraums im Plural endweder nur maskuline Formen oder auch neben diesen gleichfalls feminine Genusmorpheme bei sich haben können und letztere in mehr oder weniger starkem Maße bevorzugen; dise Substantive werden hier als "hetrogene" (früher von uns auch weniger glücklich, aber dem Sprachgebrauch vor allem für das Rumänische angepaßt "ambigene") bezeichnet.", ibid, p. 213.
[4] S. Frashëri, *Shkronjëtore e gjuhës shqip* (1886), Vepra 2, Tiranë, 1988, p. 105.

Latin language in its appearance[5]. There were two factors[6], which according to him, brought to the appearance of this phenomenon: disappearance of limit line of the gender of the nouns of non animated beings, and the analogy.

Two-gender noun phenomenon was more common in the North Dialect (Geg), thus proven from the time of old authors, whereas in Tosk Dialect it was introduced later. Being a phenomenon which was spread all over the Albanian country, the two-gender noun phenomenon was accepted as normative in standard language. But different language researchers, those before the standardization of the Albanian language and after that, had and still are having different attitude towards this respective issue. Among the linguists who were against the acceptance of the two-gender norm, or who have expressed the problems which would bring the application of the norm in using the adjectives that accompany nouns in plural of this category, are; Gj. Pekmezi, J. Rrota, S. Riza, A. Dhrimo[7], and lately R. Memushaj[8].

Gjergj Pekmezi in his grammar book keeps with consistency masculine gender, e.g. *ujëra të mire, të mirë ujëra, male të lartë, të lartë male* (Gj. Pekmezi p.117-119)[9]. There is another northern author, S. Riza, who does not accept two-gender phenomenon, thus introducing, e.g; **kontributet madhorë; tre kontributet më të mëdhenj; të teksteve të vjetër** (S. Riza p. 20, 233, 243)[10]. But even today when the two-gender phenomenon has been accepted as a norm, we often encounter wrong gender accord, for e.g.: **këta kushte, këta djathëra, të gjithë drithërat, gjithë elementet e tjerë, drithëra të pjekur** etc.

Later on, A. Dhimo, one of the authors who was engaged more with adjectives, expresses his opinion that 'it wouldn't be a mistake if written language would

---

[5] *Sh. Demiraj, Rreth Ndërrimit të gjinisë së emrave në shumës në gjuhën shqipe vështruar edhe në përqasje me rumanishten, SF, nr. 4, Tiranë, 1968, p. 83-96.*
[6] *Ibid p. 93.*
[7] Vide: Gj. Pekmezi, *Grammatik der albanesischen Sprache,* Wien, 1908, p.119; J. Rrota, *Gjuha e shkrueme ase vërejtje gramatikore,* Botime Françeskane, Shkodër, 2006, p. 134; S. Riza, *Vepra të zgjedhura,* ASHSH/QSA, Tiranë, 2009, p. 21; A. Dhrimo, *Për shqipen dhe shqiptarët 1,* Infbotues Tiranë, 2008, p. 62 - 64.
[8] Vide: R. Memushaj *Për shqipen standarde* 1, Infbotues, Tiranë, 2012, p. 101 - 103.
[9] Gjergj Pekmezi, *Grammatik der Albanesischen Sprache,* Verlag des Albanesischen Vereines, Wien, 1908, p. 117-119.
[10] S. Riza, *Vepra të zgjedhura,* ASHSH/QSA, Tiranë, 2009, p. 20, 233, 243.

keep with consistency masculine gender in plural for all types of masculine nouns[11].

Regarding these objections and suspicion, in this commentary we will take a hold at the synchronic aspect of this phenomenon, in a modest attempt to point out difficulties of two-gender noun accord with adjectives, pronouns and numerals, whether they are introduced in the function of determiners, or when they are used in anaphoric and predicative function in a sentence or a compound clause. The difficulty of accord is found in spoken as well as in written language.

During the research of this phenomenon in newspapers, scripts and different texts, gender accord of two-gender nouns with determiners comes out to be more and more frequent problem because of the mistakes in linking the determined word with determiners.

Thus, there are a lot of examples about this usage: *materiale **elektrikë**, nuk ka male më **të lartë**, ..., , fshatra **fushorë**, lista e elementeve **kimikë**, ..., ka shumë monumente **historikë** që kanë mbërritur në ditët tona, Ikea do të shesë panele **diellorë** në Britaninë e Madhe! I ftohti izolon më tej fshatrat **malore të mbuluar** nga dëbora, Fakte dhe dokumente **historikë** që dëshmojnë lidhjen e Ismail Qemalit* ...etc. These two-gender nouns should have had the determiners of feminine gender like: *male më të larta* (higher mountains), *fshatra fushore/malore* (field/mountain villages), *elemente kimike* (chemical elements) *monumente historike* (historical monuments), *panele diellore* (solar panels) *dokumente historike* (historical documents).

This is not all as far as the two – gender problems are concerned. In different articles and in everyday speech we have noticed movement of gender accord of many nouns which are not two-gender, such as *kuadër* (staff), *teatër* (theatre) etc. These nouns of masculine gender are not two-gender nouns, however in plural we find them used suchlike, giving them determiners of feminine gender: *New staff* (kuadrot e reja) *were stopped to become part of the personnel. Kosovo Railways has been investing in new staff* (kuadrot e reja);

---

[11] A. Dhrimo, *Për shqipen dhe shqiptarët*, vëll. 1, Infbotues, Tiranë, p. 62.

new managing staff (kuadrot e reja)*; there was necessity of new for new professional staff* (kuadro të reja): *Going to Kuç was welcome by the managing staff* (kuadro të reja) *The first staff* (kuadrot e reja) *of Albanian language) were trained in this school* etc. The same happens the noun *teatër* (theatre), *e.g. Borovci is doing her job in on of the most famous theatres* (teatrove) *in Pitsburg. Three performances in oie of well-known theatres* (teatrove) *in Paris* etc. Both these nouns, in plural as well, should be determined by word determined adjectives in masculine gender, because they do not form plural either by – *e* or by – *ra*. So it should be*: New staff* (kuadro të rinj) *managing staff* (kuadro drejtues), *professional staff* (kuadro profesionistë), *first staff* (kuadrot e pare) *etc., or in one of well-known theatres* (teatrot e njohur), *well-known theatres* (teatrot e njohur).

Apart from the above mentioned nouns, there are other masculine nouns which are not two-gender, mainly nouns which form plural by adding the suffix –**a**, especially when the stem ends in –**r**, e.g.: *brez* (generation) - *breza, gol* (goal) - *gola, gërshet* (pig-tail) - *gërsheta, hap* (step) - *hapa, interes* (interest) - *interesa, libër* (book) - *libra, nerv* (nerve) - *nerva, mekanizëm* (mechanism) - *mekanizma, organizëm* (organism) *organizma, rresht* (row) - *rreshta, tip* (type) - *tipa, term* (term) - *terma* etc. appear as two-gender in both forms of speech e.g. *edhe **interesat kombëtare,** edhe BE-në; Gruevski bëri thirrje për bashkim për **interesat shtetërore dhe nacionale;**...është një nga objektivat e auditorit.......në përmbushjen e objektivave të parapara; u përuruan **librat e botuara**[12]. Qeveria ka marrë vendim për rishikimin e **të gjitha librave, të cilat** nxisin ndasi dhe urrejtje. Ai tha se **librat e reja** të historisë në Kosovë do të jenë **të gatshme**.... **të gjitha organizmatt e gjalla** kanë qeliza......Ajo kërkon që qeveria të forcojë **të gjitha mekanizmat** për të siguruar zbatim të saktë; flok/flokë; Debati i pardjeshëm në Komisionin e ligjeve ishte padyshim një spektakël i tepërt, një episode bajat, ku **nervat e lodhura** flasin me zë të lartë; **lekë të reja; lekë të vjetra; Termat e përdorura** në këtë statut kanë të njejtin kuptim me ato të*

---

[12] Even Sami Frasheri, himself, makes a mistake putting into this category the word **emër** "ca emra meshkuj të cilavet, këto emra" (some male names which, these names) which make the plural not by – **ra,** but by – **a** (plural morphem).

5

përcaktuara në nenin 2 të ligjit .....; ***Termat e vjetra*** *bartin në vetvete lashtësinë*
.....; *hoqi* ***petkat e bardha; petkat tradicionale;*** *Jam i lumtur me* ***golat e***
shenuara; *Këtu mund t'i shikoni shtatë* ***golat e shenuara*** *në ndeshjen ndërmjetë*
dy ekipeve; ***Këto*** *janë disa tipe* ***të cilat*** *gjenden rrallë* ....etc. We find this
obstruction even in nouns which make the plural by adding other suffixes, such
as: *flok* (hair), *lek* (lek), *sy* (eye): *Albana has got long hair; In the late '70-ies a*
man with long hair used to move along in Tirana; fair hair; Open black eyes
(title of a song); 17 thousand new leks for a scanner etc.

In all these cases one-gender masculine nouns in plural are used in a wrong
way with determiners of feminine gender. In these sentences, adjectives and
pronouns have to be of masculine gender, as when they are in a function of a
determiner of a syntagma, as well as in an anaphoric or predicative function.
E.g.: *interesat kombëtatë* (national interest);*interesat shtetërorë* (state interest);
njëri nga objektivat (one of the objectives);*..e të gjithë librave, të cilët* (of all
books, which)....*librat e rinj* (new books) *librat e botuar* (published books); *të*
gjithë organizmat (all organisms): *nervat e lodhur* (weakened nerves); *termat e*
vjetër (old terms); *flokë të gjatë* (long hair); *golat e shënuar* (scored goals);
lekë të rinj/të vjetër (old/new leks); *këto janë disa tipe*[13]*, që* ... (these are several
types that...) etc.

Wrong gender accord occurs not only when a two-gender masculine noun in
plural and the word which determines it are within a syntagma, but also when
they are in distance (in anaphoric and predicative function). Not only ordinary
speakers make a mistake in this case, but also speakers who have been
linguistically formed. Except adjectives there are also some pronouns which
have accord problems, e.g.: *i cili (which), njëri-tjetri (one another)* as in the
example: *Modulet plotësojnë* ***njëra - tjetrën*** *me një përzierje nxitëse të*

---

[13] Plural of the noun **tip** (type) (according to the norm, **tip/a**) in written is often introduced with
shaping morpheme-**e**. In this case the mistake is not only in plural, but mistakes continue as
chain reaction in accord with other members which this noun is linked to, in a compound
sentence as well, In our case, the pronoun whose gender is introduced in a wrong way, so it has
to be of masculine gender. Te same occurs with the noun **term** (according to the norm, **term/a**)
which in written and spoken form is often introduced by
–**e**, term/e (terms).

letërsisë... (Modules complete **one another** with a challenging mix of the literature...) <u>*Manifestimet*</u> *për dëshmorët e kombit dallojnë nga* **njëra - tjetra** ... (Manifestation for the national martyrs differ from **one another**....)*; Eurozona formohet nga 17 vende anëtare, të cilat kanë madhësi dhe kushte të ndryshme nga njëra - tjetra (*Euro zone was constituted out of 17 state **members, which** differ in size and conditions from **one another**); Padyshim dy <u>regjimet</u> janë të ngjashme **me njëra - tjetrën** (There is no doubt both regimes are **similar** to **one another**)*; Sistemet janë të ngjashme* **me njëra - tjetrën** (Systems are **independent** from **one another**); *Këto* <u>*koncepte*</u> *janë të lidhura ngushtë* **me njëra - tjetrën** (These concepts are tightly linked with **one another**); *Në ligjin që është në fuqi, ka dy* <u>nene,</u> *të cilat nuk janë në harmoni* **me njëra - tjetrën** (In the law which is in power, there are two articles, **which** are not in accordance with **one another**)*; Duke pasur parasysh marrëdhëniet në mes të* <u>dy shteteve,</u> *të cilat ende nuk e kanë njohur* **njëra - tjetrën** ... (Considering the relations between two countries, **which**, still have not recognized **one another**....) etc.

In the above mentioned examples there are two-gender nouns: *koncepte* (concepts), *module* (modules), *manifestime* (manifestations), *regjime* (regimes), *sisteme* (systems), *nene (*articles)*, shtete* (states), *vende* (places), which are determined by adjectives and pronouns of feminine gender which have the function of a determiner, of anaphoric and predicative function, whose gender accord with two-gender noun is wrong. Indefinite pronoun ***njeri-tjetri*** (one another) changes the plural of the above mentioned nouns into singular. (*njëri modul e plotëson modulin tjetër* "one module completes the other module"*; dy nene që nuk janë në harmoni me njëri tjetrin* "two articles which are not in accordance with one another") the same happens with the other examples. So, the adjective in predicative function as well as the relative pronoun ***të cilët*** *(which)* in anaphoric function have to be of masculine gender, e.g. : *Modules complete one another....17 state members which differ in size and conditions from one another; These concepts are tightly linked to one another.... two states, which still haven't recognized one another* etc.

Frequent movements are also found when we use indefinite pronouns, *njëri, asnjëri (one, noone)* when linked with a two-gender noun, e.g.: *Gjilani është njëra nga shtatë qytetet më të mëdha të Kosovës* (Gjilan is one of the seven biggest cities in Kosova); *Ai shprehet i bindur se asnjëra nga konkluzionet e Coopoer-it nuk e prekin siovranitetin e Kosovës* (He is convinced that none of Cooper's conclusions affect Kosova's sovereignty) etc. In the above mentioned sentences gender accord is wrong, because the pronoun *njëri, (or no one of the two things or notions)*, in this case, shows only one thing or notion, out of two ore few things or notions of the same type[14]. So this pronoun has to be of masculine gender, because nouns, *qytete* (cities), *konkluzione* (conclusions), in singular are of masculine gender, e.g. (*njëri qytet nga shtatë qytetet dhe asnjëri konkluzion nga konkluzionet e dhëna).*

As we pointed out, above obstruction of the norm, we encounter not only in spoken language but in written language as well, and not only among ordinary speakers without language background (illiterate people or those with only primary education), but also with speakers with language culture and a lot of experience in writing, or even some linguists who make mistakes mentioned above. Such facts prove that the norm of acco of determiners' accord with two-gender nouns is still far from its clearance, and that the acceptance of the two-gender phenomenon has made the issue more complicated.

Difficulties revealed by determiners' accord with a two-gender noun has drawn linguists' attention. Thus, Father J. Rrota has pointed out the problems that have to do with two-gender phenomenon, when a two-gender noun has many adjective determiners, as in the examples like: *Mali më i lartë i të gjitha të tjerave të Shqipnis âshtë Tomori[15].*

Lately the linguist R. Memushaj, has returned to the two-gender phenomenon. He referred to it in order to show that the unification of grammatical norms implicates a long historical process, during which there has to be made a careful

---

[14] ASHSH, *Gramatika e gjuhës shqipe*, 1, Tiranë, 2002, p. 253.
[15] J. Rrota, *Gjuha e shkrueme ase vërejtje gramatikore,* Botime Françeskane, Shkodër, 2006, p. 194.

balance among all factors, those in favor and those against a certain choice between two competitive forms.

Comparing the examples with and without two-gender nouns, where terms that are linked with a nominal syntagma which has as a head a two-gender noun, belong to a verbal or another inflectional syntagma (to a sentence) as: *Këto male të larta* vështrojnë *njëri-tjetrin* and *Këto male të larta* vështrojnë *njëra-tjetrën; Këto male të larta të cilat i rrinë përkrah njëri-tjetrit,* and *Këto male të larta të cilat i rrinë përkrah njëra-tjetrës,* this author points out syntactic problems which derive from the two-gender phenomenon.

According to him, the first way seems to be more acceptable, but the principle of the linking theory, according to which the anaphoric pronoun is linked to a preceding word in the same sentence, is broken. And this means that the anaphoric pronoun *njëri-tjetri (one another)* needs a preceding word in plural and in masculine gender, while the preceding word *malet (mountains)* is in feminine gender. The second way complies with the principle of the linking theory since the preceding word *malet (mountains)* and the anaphoric pronoun *njëri-tjetri (one another)* too, are in feminine gender. But the pronoun *njëri-tjetri (one another)* as a mutual pronoun implies nouns of feminine gender, while the noun *mal (mountain)* is of masculine gender. From what we have discussed in this part, it comes out that this author is also against the acceptance of the two-gender phenomenon as a norm, though he is not clear about this.

Another factor which complicates gender accord is also the problematic issue of plural of a lot of nouns. We find the treatment of this issue in the work *"Për shqipen standarde"* of the author R. Memushaj, who points out the swing of plural of nouns and plural oscillation between vocabularies and grammar. Here is also pointed out the plural of few nouns, which gets out of morphological system, e.g.: *teatro* (theatre*),* kuadro (staff), *amfiteatro* (amphitheatre), *kinoteatro* (cinema theatre), *kabllo* (cable) {in *Fjalori i gjuhës shqipe, 2006},* but Memushaj is right, when he introduces the plural of these nouns with – **a: *kuadra, teatra, amfiteatra, kinoteatra, kabla***[16], because considers the word formation morpheme of plural, **-o**, as a strange one for Albanian language[17]. This discord between normative vocabularies and the norm given by normative grammar put even more influence in disorientation of speakers about the gender accord of nouns with determining words.

As a conclusion, we can say that the two-gender phenomenon is a phenomenon which not only points out disorientation in gender accord of two-gender nouns with **–e** and **–ra**, and determining words (adjectives, pronouns and numerals), but which analogically includes other nouns that do not belong to the two-gender ones. After all, this phenomenon does not come out to be in function of any language parameter which plays an important grammatical role.

To say it openly, the two-gender phenomenon does not bring any benefit to Albanian language, but on the contrary, it makes problems in according the terms of syntagmas, noun + adjective, noun + pronoun, pronoun + noun, numeral + noun, especially when the

latest ones come out in anaphoric and predicative functions in a sentence. We think that it would have been better for the norm of Albanian language if these nouns (two-gender) in plural had been determined by determiners of masculine gender.

---

[16] A. Dhimo, R. Memushaj, *Fjalori drejtshkrimor i gjuhës shqipe,* Infbotues, Tiranë;, 2011 f. 396, 806, 19, 329, 361.
[17] R. Memushaj, *Për shqipen standarde 1,* Infbotues, Tiranë, f. 61 - 69.

Resume

The use of two-gender nouns is a language phenomenon which appears in some indoeuropiane languages and which has for a long time attracted the attention of linguists. This phenomenon appears in languages such as: Italian, French, Rumanian, Slovakian, Czech and Albanian.

In each of these languages, nouns of this class appear as masculine in singular, but when they become plural they appear in feminine gender. This phenomenon is known as the usage of two-gender nouns. Nouns which are included in the class of two-gender nouns mainly name in animates, objects or abstract notion, as for ex.: *element/i – element/e, vend/i – vend/e, qytet/i n- qytet/e, kryeqytet/i – kryeqytet/e, breg/u – brigj/e, lloj/i – lloj/e, send/i – sende/e, djep/i – djep/i - djep/e, etc.; vaj/i – vaj/e, fshat/i – fshat/ra, drith-ë/i – drithëra, uj-ë/i – ujëra, lesh/i – leshra, mall/i – mallra, të qeshura* etc. There are also a few ther nouns which belong to this class and that name animaties as for ex.: *personazh – personazhe, ekuipazh – ekuipazhe, personalitet – personalitete, ekip – ekipe, insekt – insekte, bakter – baktere, virus – viruse, mikrob – mikrobe* etc. So, Albanian language two-gender nouns appear as masculine, (a group of which have originally been neutral), which form the plural with the inflectional suffixes **–e** and **–ra.**

There are several linguists who opposed the acceptance of two-gender nouns as a standard and some others who have pointed out the problems that follow if the standard of adjective usage that accompany nouns in plural of this class is applied. These are: Gj. Pekmezi, S. Riza, A. Dhrimo, J. Rrota and recently R. Memushaj.

On the research of this phenomenon in the newspapers, pieces of writing and different texts, the agreement in gender of ambiguous nouns with determiners are grammatically wrongly adapted to their gender. The wrong adaptation in gender happens when this linking is in contact with the sintagma (phrase) parts as well as in distance (in the anaphoric and predicate function). There are also

11

some pronouns which cause problems in adapting, for ex. **i cili, njëri-tjetri**, as for ex.: *Modulet plotësojnë **njëra-tjetrën** me një përzierje nxitëse të letrësisë....; *Manifestimet për dëshmorët e kombit dallojnë nga **njëra-tjetra**.; *Eurozona formohet nga 17 vende anëtare, **të cilat** kanë madhësi dhe kushte të ndryshme nga **njëra-tjetra**.*

We often find instability during the usage of non-defined pronouns **njëri, asnjëri**, when they are linked with a two-gender noun, ex. *Gjilani është njëra nga shtatë qytetet e mëdha të Kosovës...; *Ai shprehet I bindur se asnjëra nga konluzionet e Cooperit nuk e prekin sovranitetin e Kosovës* etc.

Some authors do the opposite. They define the two-gender nouns by using words that belong to masculine gender, as for ex.: *ujëra të mire, male të lartë, të lartë male* (Gj. Pekmezi, pg.117-119); *kontributet madhorë, tre kontributet më të mëdhenj, teksteve të vjetër* (S. Riza, pg. 20, 233, 243) etc. S. Riza uses this phenomenon deliberately.

But the problems that are caused by two-gender usage do not end here. In different pieces of work we have noticed vibration in adaption with quite a lot of two-gender nouns, as for ex.: *kuadër/kuadro, teatër/teatro* etc. these nouns belong to masculine gender according to the standard but in different pieces of writing and in the spoken language are used as two-gender nouns, i.e are defined by feminine determiners, as in the example: * **Kuadrot e reja** stopohen që të jenë pjesë e stafit...; *Hekurudhat e Kosovës po investojnë në **kuadrot e reja; kuadrot e reja drejtuese**.*

According to the research we have made, except the above-mentioned nouns, it derives that the analogy has also effected other masculine nouns to appear as two-gender ones, both in the written and spoken language, as for example: *interes / interesa, libër / libra, nerv / nerva, term / terma, gërshet / gërsheta, brez / breza, organizëm / organizma, petk / petka, rresht /rreshta, hap / hapa, mekanizëm / mekanizma; tre {m} / tri {f} (tre djem, tri vajza) gol/gola, flok/flokë, mikroorganizëm / mikroorganizma, tip / tipa, rresht / rreshta, numër /numra* etc.

Another factor that complicates the adaptation in gender is also the problematic issue of the plural of a lot of nouns. We find a treatment for this issue in the work *"Për shqipen standarde"* by R. Memushaj, who righteously points out vibration of the plural of the few nouns and differences of the given plurals in dictionaries and grammars. It's worth to point out here the plural of same nouns which doesn't fit with the morphology system, as for ex. *teatro, amfiteatro, kinoteatro, kabllo* (in Dictionary of Albanian Language, 2006); whereas Memushaj gives righteously the plural of these nouns with –**a**: *kuadra, amfiteatra, kinoteatra, kablla,* because the inflation morpheme of the plural with –**o** according to him is unknown for Albanian.

As a conclusion we can say that the use of two gender nouns presents a phenomenon that not only points out disorientation in the adaption of the gender two gender nouns with –**e** and –**ra** and of defining words (adjectives, pronouns and numerals), but using analogy is also including the which are not two gendered.

Bibliography

ASHSH, *Fjalori i gjuhës së sotme shqipe*, Tiranë, 2006.

ASHSH, *Gramatika e gjuhës shqipe 1*, Tiranë, 2002.

Buhholz, O., Fiedler, W., *Albanische Grammatik*, Verlag Enzyklopädie, Leipzig, 1987.

Demiraj, Sh., *Rreth ndërrimit të gjinisë së emrave në shumës në shqipe vështruar edhe në përqasje me rumanishten*, SF, nr. 4, Tiranë, 1968.

Dhrimo A., Memushaj R., *Fjalor drejtshkrimor i gjuhës shqipe*, Infbotues, Tiranë, 2011.

Dhrimo, A., *Për shqipen dhe shqiptarët*, I, Infbotues, Tiranë, 2008.

http://www.de.wikipedia.org/wiki/Genus#Ambigeneratjen.

Frashëri, Sami, *Shkronjëtore e gjuhës shqip* (1886), Vepra 2, Tiranë, 1988.

Fiedler, Wilfried, *Die Pluralbildung im Albanischen*, ASHAK, Prishtinë, 2007.

Memushaj, R. *Për shqipen standarde I*, Infbotues, Tiranë, 2011.

Pekmezi, Gj., *Albanesische Grammatik*, Wien, 1908.

Prifti, S., *Sintaksa e gjuhës shqipe*, Prishtinë, 1971.

Riza, S., *Vepra të zgjedhura*, ASHSH/QSA, Tiranë, 2009.

Rrota, J., *Gjuha e shkrueme ase vërejtje gramatikore*, Botime Françeskane, Shkodër, 2006.

14

YOUR KNOWLEDGE HAS VALUE